Strange Tales from Cherokee Street

Edited by

Daniel W. Wright and Mack Thorn

Spartan Press

Spartan Press

Kansas City, MO

spartanpress.com

Spartan
Press

Acknowledgments

Special thanks to Spartan Press, Spine Bookstore and Cafe, Joe's Cafe, Barb's Books, Osage Arts Community, O'Connell's Pub, Dunaway Books, Schlafly's Taproom, CBGB's, The Bookhouse, The Crow's Nest, The Whiskey Ring, The B-Side, and Fortune Teller Bar and the denizens of Cherokee Street.

Table of Contents

Daniel W. Wright

Jim McGowin

Denmark Laine

Jessie Eikmann

S. Elizabeth Cook

Mack Thorn

Dedicated to the cast members of the epic,
live-streaming public-access surreality show
that is Cherokee Street, St. Louis, MO, USA.

Well the barrooms close at two A.M. in St. Louis
And I'm always the last one out the door
There's at least a hundred barrooms in St. Louis
And I've tried them all a dozen times or more

-Johnny Paycheck, "Spirits of St. Louis"

Strange Tales from
Cherokee Street

Daniel W. Wright

Daniel W. Wright is an award-nominated poet and fiction writer. He most recently wrote the foreword for *Sacred Decay: The Art of Lauren Marx* (Dark Horse, 2021). He is the author of eight collections of poetry, including *Love Letters from the Underground* (Spartan Press, 2021), *Rodeo of the Soul* (Spartan Press, 2019), and *Murder City Special* (Bad Jacket, 2017). His work has appeared in print journals such as *The Literary Parrot, BUK100, 365 Days,* and *Gasconade Review*, as well as online journals such as *Book of Matches*. He currently resides in St. Louis, MO, where you can usually find him in a bar or a bookstore.

Kingdom of Mud

The beginning isn't always
the best place to start
The ego is never the truth
Those who follow in blind faith
never know where they're going
Pretty tales in Merry Land
set sail
without letting anyone know
Ribbons left from better days
still hang on through the dark clouds

Railroads are a paper trail
to anywhere else
The world finally got over
the second World War
but it still has a lifetime of therapy
ahead of it
History lessons by word of mouth
are always more interesting
than anything you can learn
in a book

Does it matter
what they really call you,
so long
as they call you King?
They're all so regal
walking with a six pack
and sense of self-worth

Those who look up
have much to worry about
Those who look down
don't care
No one dies alone
so we all cry the same
A long way from secret dreams
most are too scared to take
Hours spent daydreaming
of better lives we all deserve

If Mark Twain didn't say
half the shit he gets credit for
does that mean
that shit is up for grabs?
Drove an academic insane
All I did was speak plain
Ghosts want to bury you
when they see you climb out
They shed a tear
when they hear
that nobody wants
to make love
to a memory motel

The truce of twilight
is always a false flag
The lights of the carnival
are too much after awhile
Yelling at a hall of mirrors
because someone has to take the blame

Too many mad as hell
and not gonna take it anymore
The organ grinder tries to drive
everyone else
to his point of insanity

Someone will set
another Great Fire
just to give the rest of us
a story to tell
Crescendo strings let you know
it's time to go

So Well Read

Like most guys
who fancy themselves
a smarty pants
there sits on my bookshelf
a copy of *Infinite Jest*
that I know
I will never try to read

But it looks good

Never Trust an Off Brand Pizza Roll

There are certain things in life
you just don't do
You don't tug on Superman cape
You don't spit in the wind
You don't mess with Slim
And you never trust
an off-brand pizza roll

In my many years
in this crazy little thing called life,
I have never met an off-brand pizza roll
that didn't either piss my stomach off
for at least a day,
taste like soggy shit,
or both.

At this point,
if I were faced with hunger
or eating an off-brand Pizza Roll,
I would choose hunger
Now, that may sound
at first glance
like hyperbole.
But I would rather be hungry
than deal with my stomach yelling,
"Why did you make that life choice?!"
and then punishing me
with a seemingly never ending

intestinal pressure
unlike anything else
on this planet
Yeah, I'll chose hunger
over that

11:11

Make a wish just for a minute
and hope that it comes true
Ice turns the tea
to flavored water
An honest life is never seen
until after the fact

Cigarette leans against the pillar
in a white shirt and a baseball cap
It knows it's got a bad habit
But consequences
are never meant
for today

.

Trieste

The weather is perfect.
West coast winds cool
midwestern insecurities
The jukebox is playing
"My Favorite Things" by John Coltrane.
I'm enjoying a cup of coffee
while reading the poems of others
and writing a few of my own.
I don't know if there is a Heaven,
but this is pretty fucking close.

Screamadelic

At the crossroads of my soul
at the edge of American Dreams
I now know what I want for myself
but I need to wait a little longer
to see who all is in it with me
Minding the gap
and not letting myself down
where yesterday calls home

Psychedelic soundtrack symphony
sitting in the park
stoned
Feeling evolutions
show love for thyself
Pacific Ocean breezes
clear the hesitation
to show a dream can be done
All that is needed
is the will to walk the way

Still

Running to stand still
Mother Nature steps in
when we can't take the hint
I sit cross-legged
while the world makes up
for lost crazy
Hide in peace and lay still
to feel your skin
Your heart moving you
back and forth
like a sea shanty
to the road of sobriety
as stillness leads to clarity
Like bubbles blowing in the breeze
we shall go
where we need to be

Zero Fucks

"I give no fucks!"
they'll say as a verbal flex
But if they gave no fucks
they wouldn't feel a need
to shout
that they gave no fucks
Some even dare to say
"I don't give an F"
But they do
If they care enough
to not actually say the word
Fuck
Then they must care something
in regards of a supposed decency
in addition to announcing to the world
so, they can let the world know
that they have
zero fucks

They'll repeat the phrase enough times
so that every stranger
in shouting distance knows
They'll shout every agro nu metal chorus
that states this mantra
to display a perceived individuality
They'll know they're the alpha
in every room they enter
because they have let every possible person

they have met in this world
which realistically
may only account for
at best
.07% of the population
But they'll know
that those people know
that they give
no fucks

They'll tattoo it on their forehead
They'll tattoo it on their leg
They'll tattoo it on their bicep
right underneath the barbed wire tat
So it can be visible for the world to see
that they are a cut above
because they don't give
one
single
lousy
fuck

For The Ones Who Used to Love Us

The ones who now have kids
and the lives they always wanted
when we were all younger
once upon a time
Who saw our special something
before we even did

The ones who cried with us
when things broke off
because they saw the journey
we had to go on
and knew
they couldn't go with us

Who still love us
because we have found comfort
in our own skin
and tell us how proud they are
whenever they see us
They are the ones we loved truly
once upon a time

History Never Repeats but It Often Rhymes

Fog covers the houses on the hill
just enough to make them seem
like a mirage
A man punching the strings
of a chipped guitar
sees me putting on my face mask
and screams,
"Nobody knows you when you're unknown!"

New blazer goofin'
to feel more like myself
Palm trees put on their shades
to blast yacht rock
from their convertible Cadillacs
with Deadhead stickers
on the bumpers
Whole Foods in the good part of town
lets you know the avocados
will keep you safe

Tickets to the soon-to-open
wheel in space
will be affordable too little too late
John Mayer blasts the yuppie dreams
for Millennials

Good ideas
afraid to come out to play

because they don't want
to be bought, sold, and distorted
Giving a meal I bought
to a bum who asked me for a dollar
He needed it more than me
Nobody wins
unless we all get in it
together

Mother's Day in the Checkout Lane

Went to the supermarket
on Mother's Day
The woman in front of me
at checkout
had a gallon of vodka
a Lean Cuisine
and a stuffed bunny
Some questions
are better left unanswered

Watching a Master at Work

(for Neeli Cherkovski)

Sitting next to a literary idol
watching him read
for college students
Watching a master spin his spells
smiling as I learn how to be better
Fan boy impulses kept in check
with questions waiting behind the velvet rope

He reads his elegies
and tells to hang on to the Yangtze River
I take in the blur of a moment
that seems unreal
when it is over
and I hope I didn't overstay my welcome
I've been told to never meet my heroes
I guess I've lucked out so far
and met all the right ones

There You Go Again

When an absolute lays on your lips
do you dare speak it?
Labyrinths test trust
when the journey is so long
what does one do
when the destination arrives
Blue water crashing upon each other
call the mad pirates home

Sometimes the only way to go
is that which ain't right
but ain't exactly wrong
The pain of the right way to go
will never be more
than one can bare
if you dare to seek
the last lightning bolt

Mad Gods and Midwestern Gentlemen

The river is a mad god
that grabs you by his red right hand
to offer you a Faustian deal
for a life's supply of snake oil

Any man of confidence knows
that mice and flies
won't fall for the same traps anymore
but they'll always be led to poison

Compassion is a devil's game
Every sinner has to leave paradise
because in the long term
none of us can afford it

The Wave

Yearning for another man's nostalgia
when reading about
where the wave finally broke
Feeling the traces of an oasis
just out of reach in time
Some still await
for the wave to come back to shore

Even if another does roll in
it will never be as it was
Though those who forget history
are doomed to repeat it
It will different
as different as two snowflakes
Similar to the naked eye
But different once you stop
and really take a look

Hopefully five steps forward
will not be followed
by six steps back
Hopefully solutions will be offered
instead of more questions
Hopefully a wave will come again
in our lifetime

Jim McGowin

Jim McGowin has a background in media communications and visual art. He prefers to create cool stuff, but keeps a day job. His poems have been published in *Chance Operations, The UCity Review, Rusty Truck* and *The Gasconade Review*. He is the author of several chapbooks of poetry and the collection *Murmuration*, published in 2018 by Spartan Press. He lives in St. Louis, Missouri with his family and two cats.

Icarus Ritual

Who ever heard of someone dying upon returning from the sky?

Making a mockery of the shadow that arises to cradle them -

Throwing back blue curtains,
a malfunction of branched and linked edges,
breathing sounds in lunatic haste.

A fetching hoax (do not deny it),
sparkling in the lusty dark.
The unfolding euphoria is foolish -
it comes on the day of the week
when the light wears out its welcome,

Charmed by pinnacles, and snared in an Icarus ritual.

> We all look for comfort
> in revelations and knells,
> trying hard to be just and do well.
> But the most curious charms
> are the ones that do harm,
> raising questions, and
> chaos and hell.

Falling in desperation is an underrated way to get anywhere.

Abscissions

Once
I thought I knew the wound,
could trace its outline like open lips
whispering my own voice
back to me,
like a trail stumbles in familiar half-sleep.

Once
I thought the wound spoke my name
back to me,
as a dream speaks to awakening,
convinced by faulty hallucinations.

Once
I thought the wound was in each throat,
a harmony of one word, one fortune,
but my tongue was rebuffed and cryptic,
language was no longer so obvious,
sealed within the stitch of a whisper.

Once
I thought…
But I was wrong –
it was only the falseness in a fable,
where the wind might tend to go, into
the slow exhale of giving something up,

A crumbling mouth and wretched
heap of abscissions,

The ability to scream
without raising any suspicion.

Bad Weather Patterns

The stun of the sun's armor in embers,
a naked cage of crestfallen bone, sobbing blue
with a séance voice built of turbulent pillows,
impure sleep suffocating kisses and throbbing marrow,
disrobing the abstraction of grey from death's sober hue.

Will-o-the-wisp, stark and thirsty, a stubborn buckling
in my own narrow voice, quipped into a distraction about
reaching the clouds too late to be a wounding arrow,
the hand drawn back in confused indecision,
bereft of any Elysian infection or crimson dew.

The sky, a stalking dome with its claw tips burning,
waiting for the tender yearn of parting skin,
a predator's praise for the prey's complicit turning,
the tempest hawk to the crystalline dove,
contorted in a perversion of flirtation and love.

Little doldrum death, shivering with lightning's blow,
copulating hammers din in a funeral full of nail holes,
erecting a hail-carved effigy and howling storm gale,
beating the dermis mad into submissive disintegration,
a last chrome of sweat, spilling bitter and waxing pale.

Frenzy blooms and wilts into a ruin of arms and legs,
a blanch of broken stone bodies, subdued of any context,
beguiled by bad weather patterns, the primordial disease,

a mote of spurned fingers reaching forever perplexed,
assailing and predictable, into the mind's cloudy eye,
the tearful hope of an awakening teased,
in the empty embrace of a ruthless night's breeze.

Abominable Muse

It's always on an obligatorily dim street,
with arsenic tones of wet skin and crude meat,
where a villainy of amoral exploits will win,
the crisis of rubbish, a crucifix cheek turned
to mercenary grin, synonymous with the bigger mess -
the abominableness of me, I must confess.

Hold tight to your gutter-sham opus and rambles,
your compromised candles, sincerest of lights,
lest I blow them all out like a birthday curse,
a quaint childish wish, only paid in reverse.
Each ardent virtue shall be tempted astray
through a sanctified door, to a debauched foray,
so closed, so never, so near, so faint,
my temporary whore, whom I loathe and adore,
in whom flows a melodious, tortuous spoor,
fear-honed like a chance, awaiting and prone,
behind odious tomes of discord we will dance.

Steal a quick prayer for your antagonist redeemer,
the saint executioner's hatchet and stroke,
a caress and a feint by the smoke-and-mirror schemer,
standard bearer of trifles and street lamp palaver,
where too many ghosts have few words about saviors,
but plenty of poison to gratify thirst.
Indiscretion is the most cunning and subtle of burglars,
with alibis so airtight, they're destined to burst.

In the perversion of dawn on a paradoxical day,
when seeking the truth only holds you at bay,
await me in the shadows that lurk in veiled hearts,
like a path to deliverance, like a wisp in the dark,
I might pull you in close, just to lead you astray,
I might promise devotion in a quandary of verse,
you must never forget that I mean what I say -
and if I swear that I love you, I lied to you first.

Soliloquy at the Beginning and the End
of the Universe

We are really only working in the rough, scribbling out our faces in each other's peripheral vision, struggling with the nuances, trapped in the objections of our own horrible penmanship. As the days carry on in disinterested speculation about being some sort of continuum, blackmailing the prisoner's wheel will reveal no starry path to sympathy - the world only spins to make goodbye into a highly uncomfortable bed.

That being said, it is hard to know when to stop daydreaming that the sun is not the catalyst for these universal revolutions. That was our own doing, the folly of an eavesdropper to an errant conversation. Trapped in the illusion written into the eternal and peculiar circular motion of supposed blessing. Heavy is the sleepy head that falls, forever downward into a demeaning baptism, caught somewhere between aspiration and forestalling delusions, slumbering away in each pining kiss and plundered feeling, drowning in an ocean of haphazard and poor timing, like some childishly obsessive notion about rumbling clouds and silver linings.

Most will just stumble in the streets, kicking their vocalizations into the gutters, where lost incantations flounder sickly and muttering, eventually collapsing in on themselves. The more you understand gravity, the more you recognize clarity as a concave existence, an attractive framework made up of tripping hazards, like a cave dweller's superstitious insistence on throwing away wishes at passing meteors and comets.

It's enough to make you want to vomit into the cosmic toilet. But it is quite a bargain - every reincarnation comes with its own coffin. It can be quite sunny beyond your own shadow. Once illuminated, you can only hope to be alive until you're not. Maybe not this time, but quite often. The path of least resistance is the one that's least persistent. Did the Buddha say that? I'm not exactly certain.

When did you finally see through me? Was it when my eye was stuck closed like a window, an epiphany of the fragility of its own self-insistent boundaries? If you can't shatter yourself, can you truly ever know how to be open to anyone else's stream of charged particles? Breathless and out of luck, I'm exponentially all wrong, a token innuendo of uncomfortable laughter in the dark. I'm fairly certain the curtains won't gather anything but clouds. They never let the sun in to illuminate my empirical lust for some other exit. That promise was already broken when it was set in stone. See if you can guess it.

Alone, at this point I have to confess I mostly miss the escape velocity I could have found in your voice. Instead, I'm just empty enough to continue to drift in the dark void between sentences. A complete and atonal astronomical mess. An inescapable event horizon of spiraling maladdress, grasping at static and omens.

Oceans sparkle in slow motion - drifting spill... window sill... aspergil... Will the holy death of a star make sense ever again? In committing the sin of relative physics, we were the absolute worst ghosts, haunting each other just beyond the conversation, our gravitational wells bending enlightenment into a serpent-like constellation, hacked in two.

Walking between the carefully enunciated words spoken only to avoid the bite of uncertainty takes some skill. Unfortunately, the speed of light was a little too slow. In an eternity, I fell behind, reborn somewhere beyond my hypothetical conception and the last word you ever said to me:

I think it was something about the sound the universe makes when it dies.

Elegant Sigh

The reward of a silver sky goes sliding through,
to sliver the heart of the ground.
Muffled, the birds have nested in the sun,
some pious voice said, somewhere in my head, and
I'm still breathing despite a mortal blow.

An appeal of hands, carved in ambiguous flight,
lent no more than a quiet pause in the night sky.
Uneasy clouds wrought out a Pandora's Box of tears,
where some other melody was hidden,
an elegant sigh, the sigh of Hypnos finally asleep.
dreaming of my unstoppable plunge to tragedy.

Mordant wreck and pestilence raining,
reflecting the moon into the sharp edge of a rook,
disordered in dreams tangling all of my passions,
no more than a bidding, a slip into hollow fists,
pushing the wing beneath an avalanche of civil behavior,
where I am suffocating, late at night in a foggy bed,
when the irises and faint stars are pitch black and deep,

Desperate birds would whisper to sneak me into her,
hobbled and hidden in atmospheric phenomenon,
only to be lost in the contours of a fluttering breast,
like a beast turning the rewards of altitude into hostages,
exchanging them for a confession of dirt captivity.

The dreamer's dialogue does not allow vicious teeth to lapse,
as flowers drop their thorns, I feel her sincere heart turn sharply,
a subliminal tide is in the air, the shape of a primrose fragrance
or maybe the breeze of pardon from a scythe's winged path,
spilling out a ruin of red ink, enough to write
a few bleak sentences about how when she finally wakes up,
I will be the nightmare she must always forget.

Epilogue Written in Boetia

Alas I was never your poet,
I just fell through the words you gave me,
the abyss of language breaking my descent,
slashing my pages of skin into
the rumor of impractical feathers.

My lone bird was a silly thing,
hidden in your predictable prison.
I passed through your architecture like a convict
and stayed longer than my sentence required.

A freefall without light,
when you were actually the Milky Way,
the slippery scintillation of a fainting poem,
written so long ago the original star was already dead.

It never even had a name.

I listen for your tongue, feeling it in my mouth,
phonemes ascending, but actually pretending,
falling speechless and twisted,

Failing caresses lighter than eyes are remote,
averted from touching the slow arching crevasses,
and the unmistaken feeling of deceleration –
exponentially inescapable,

And so on and so forth until the very end,
the so-called epilogue,
which is always followed by a few blank pages.

The Delusion of Wearing Clothes

The ground is flat because
we insist on always standing up.

Just take away the ground -
then only our bodies.
Just take away our bodies -
then only the contoured darkness that is
forever our escort.

So be careful to not end up lost within the crowd.

Eye, without confines.
Peeled, your tastes run black.
I wear you inside my dark whereabouts.
You wear my obscured hunger for a lark.

What it must mean to be the salvation
that can never be refused, I'll never know.

Cut me out of my de rigueur attire and take what remains,
devoid of the old misunderstanding
of what is to be worn, and what is to be excised.

When I am undefined, will you finally come and fit me?
Or will you vanish into the horde, just another stitch?

The empty space always wants to put us back inside.

Is there anything without you, that isn't you?

Tenuous

Sometimes
the lies are lines and
sometimes
the lines are lies and
sometimes
the moon is nothing but a mood
hanging
in the back of the throat
suspended
by a delicate thread,
deliberately
awaiting the blade's rude
awakening.

Why I Never Listen to AM Radio

In the selective electric mythology
where nostalgia crawls and staggers
within a broken albatross' bones
stolen from their loft in the final stages
of some stupidly brazen velocity,
the splintering edges are just sharp enough
to pretend to be record player needles
that tend to skip a little too sincerely.

The Imprecision of Talking in Your Sleep

Give me another chance and
I'll show you you've been colder.
You know you are going to have to swear to it,
one of these nights.

You promised me coyly I would be rewarded
in the midst of a fairly short trance,
yet the sum of the slumber was this:

Apparently, I'm not praying to you anymore.
Not in sentences without sleep, anyway.

Not in thwarted arrangements.
Not in clever disappointments.
The unspoken wound around another night,
held down, folding burdens into ourselves,
a tangle of blanketed negotiation
when we could have had each other's messy sheets.

It's better to be mangled - fast-paced and tired out,
tried in the teeth, stuttered up and gone speechless,
as if medicine or night lights might cure our disease.

I'm a toss-and-turn prospect with lousy anesthetics.
You'll wonder if it's too cheap.
I'll wonder if it's too dangerous.

Nothing will help us regret regaining our composure.
When you're too weak, you have to turn loose.

All I ever really wanted from you was to be understood
in the context of a nap in your yesterday.

All you ever really wanted from me was to be bored.

Words Are Nothing but Carrion Birds

Methodical imposter, mourning and bare, the vulgar black bird warning in the orientation of a dead trinity.

Fill in the air with a perfectly forged copy, despite a dark and depleted nature, the tempting orgy of crossbones, axis and blue scripture.

Aerial moments spill, ill-defined shadows hurry, refined by a burning mercy that is only temporary.

Crouched in a feral hunt, stalking time's remedy - yes, it will catch its prey and eat only the heart, rending it into a twisted pile of divining rods and wishbones.

And no, it is never easy to pass through these parts, so hollow and antiquated, a conjuration of hook and binding soot, roads of imprecise knots, fleshed out with base instincts and cheap asylums to be sought.

Prodigally displayed, an imposing disturbance of skin gleefully damned and fractured in cheated breath, cursed with maximum derivation wingspan, madman impulses flowing out in enraptured mayhem.

All immodest gods will drown in their own tides, lacing cataclysm's grace with perverse proposals, connotations pantomiming a libertine's pace, with just enough taste to chase itself in a full circle, a definition of siege, flanked empty in a starving divide of alabastrine heights.

Each mechanical throat steals from its own supine rations, to fabricate a chaste purity, weary of the distortion of speaking out in unsealed corridors.

Decrypted and without their passion, words are nothing but carrion birds, the sum inadequacy of their exponential hunger, a famine spent in the wonder of ruins consumed by failed languages, ragged-winged paradoxes devouring their own nuances, scripted in irony through their own misspoken contortions.

Jackdaws

The ruin of black passerines perched
in the flawless shape of burnt notebooks.

As their blessings collapsed,
I cut even more skepticism from their ashes.

I brought out many gods,
especially the small, frightened ones.
My harbinger picked up all of their tricks,
brimming with sickle-sharp wings.

It was the loneliness found in between
vocal and scribbled warnings that
carved a coercion from a serious flight,
a substantial accomplishment
for a wrongfully exonerated dead man.

Not from madness or a murder,
but more like an unnatural crease,
a fold in the sky causing a deflection,
from a pattern-stained indigo mouth
into a multitude of voices answering
one chance question about aftermath,

And here I am, crowing on about it,
still making idle promises to the wind.

Denmark Laine:

Dreamboy#3 (A Play in No Acts)

Denmark Laine is a St. Louis poet, novelist and music critic whose work has been featured on Fox 2 KTVI, Subprimal Poetry, STL TV Live, the St. Louis Poetry Slam, *Eleven Magazine, Bad Jacket* and *Book of Matches* to name a few. He has a BFA in nothing from Southern Illinois University Edwardsville with a minor in miming and is the author of *Exile On Cherokee Street, The Gods of Autumn, Thorazine Ice Cream Parlor* and *The Absinthe Fountain*.

Dreamboy#3 (A Play in No Acts) for d.a. levy

A wall of stars or
math equations or
droplets of white paint on
the blue door?

The young knight enters in whiteface.
He wears flowers in his hatband.
He carries no sword.

DREAMBOY#3
On the heels of summer that passed like an Irish wake
I came to the blue house to look for Nora with a
suitcase full of stage names:
the Artful Dodger
Robin Hood
Tom Sawyer
Reynard
Don Quixote
Puss in Boots
Hershel   of Ostropol
Baptiste the Mime
and tried on each in turn but none pleased her.
He calls for *line.*

DEATH

I am everyone's understudy. Since shapes are mysteries
learn to wear your own.

DREAMBOY#3

Nora let the Mississippi flood her bedroom.
An empty wine glass churns in the muddy water where she
went down with the last riverboat –beloved bartenders, broken
men– who drowned themselves in corner pubs. Rambling
Joads in Springsteen denim who slept behind a 7-Eleven where
boredom cross-dresses as martyrdom, drifting round the Delta
bend on six strings calling themselves "poets of the land", born
in the mouths of catfish dead in her living room.

The part of her stepmother will be played by a pack of Virginia
Slims. Midnight cowboys who fled the suburbs to join the
rock-n'-roll circus. Nocturnal creatures burrowed so deep in
her walls she can't sleep. They break their beer cans and stamp
their feet until someone calls them "Stagger Lee." Swinger-
songwriters bluffed their way into her limelight, snuck off to
the bathroom and came out speaking in tongues to lick her
plates clean.

Seven brothers carried her uphill like the Sabine women and
grew beards to cover their guilt because they wished they had
scars,

wished they died at Little Bighorn for bragging rights, for
flashbacks of Da Nang, camped in the alley, scrounging for
compliments, mourning roadkill. They wished their daddy

was an Azusa Street panhandler washed up in a ditch with the storm crows only to drag himself onto a needle's point come payday.

Those blueblood sons of Hibbing, Minnesota adopted by the Father of Waters, up all hours talking buckshot, eased with ale, huddled for warmth around her lighter. She's wadded up every flea market troubadour like a two-dollar bill in her pocket.

Another dance for the organ grinder, another bootheel wiped on her doormat, another quid of tobacco rotting her left cheek. They fill her with a thriving weed; kudzu vine creeping through her best years choking her calendar with first dates and worthless parties, rendezvous behind the dumpster with Bowery bums and dangerous friends until there's none left but a scavenger gnawing garbage in her head. Their paw prints divide her like the Mason-Dixon while she wears their numbers on her hand like bedbugs in new cities.

Two roses are her knees. Love like driftwood tossed on the echo of their names, black sediment of years she can never wash off.

Every fare thee well that flows out every open bottle carries her alone on her raft, a mattress. Nora sinks to the bottom in her father's boots.

I ask her why am I number three?

NORA

I saw Lear in grandma's bathrobe pink as 100 plastic
flamingos, shaking storefront cages at Woolworth's that
white-knuckle the ends of MLK Drive

with a bugle that doesn't blow but when he plays you
better pay through the nose.

His fingers rattle down the keys like the L-Train
making up time and though his lips teased out a
reveille no one could hear a sound.

Tightroping the hour of the wolf, the prow of the
cement median as his thumb worries a deck of
Bicycle playing cards, fighting fraudulent dexterity he
applies fragile vibrato to the air as the tuner mumbles
'it's a bitch to find the pitch.'

With a flourish the cut hiccups three-card Monte to
crosstown traffic.

Find the lady! Find the lady!
Moab is my washpot &
YOU are my bedpan!

Cadging his nth free refill, shouldering gaunt
hipsters, Hispanic bus bench lawyers, rolling paper,
tobacco confetti, steam from manholes, ventilation
grates, TV antenna like Chinese characters parts a fry
cook from his last sawbuck & prostitutes talking like

Dante for they know what it is to wear a red camellia,
water hoses burnishing the dull pavement into a
motley of cracked mirrors, he sees it transparent in
his reflection.

DEATH
Faith tangible as sheep dung beneath your Lord's manger.

Life is also a choice of three but how come they never tire of
losing?

They tell the melting snow at their feet 'I only want to be
happy.'

I tell them 'Don't look for me, I'm yours.'

THE ROBIN
Do you see the sunrise upon my breast? Come at me, I'm
ready to ruck! I befoul all I touch! I plant my eggs, bluer
than the sky itself, in every nest of the evergreen! None can
refuse me! I steal your millet and stone fruit! I capture and
kill every earthworm in the garden! None escape me! I crack
your windowpanes! I defeat all who come near my frozen
fountain! I am the red kamikaze! The rosy wrath of winged
things! Seed-Scatterer, Berry-Hunter, Bane of Grasshoppers,
Fire itself in flight! Before the first thaw I shall die valiantly in
battle for the solstice, rip out the feathers and break the beaks
of my enemies, the Wren, the Holly King! My victory song is
an early spring!

DREAMBOY#3

Death is the lady with nothing under her clothes. The woman who owns herself, who writes ex libris wherever she walks. The one that can't be found.

The lover of all writers, she asks
DEATH
Why the vagaries? What are you so afraid of?

Is the forget-me-not so vexed in her decay? The humble discard of her splendor is the fulfillment of blue.

Look at me. No more visionary double-talk. Are they not all you? The bride you seek, the ringmaster, the professor, the young knight, the idiot child?

Your whole psychological cabaret frisking after me like a spaniel, everyone incognito (the same surly, mystic tease), whiny as any Gibran-quoter.

DREAMBOY#3
I ask her again why am I number three?

DEATH
Because we met before.

The first two times you were engrossed in some fragrant paperback bought or lifted from Barnes &

Noble to fan the flames of discontent, Sisyphus via
public transit who quit football for Shakespeare.
And your heart wasn't broken then. Useless to me.
At the periphery of everything there's a comforting
absence: Eurydice always behind your observant back, the
word in the Talmud that must not be read, the vacant
tomb in a hollow Easter chocolate, a phone number you
never call, the long wait where now and never eventually
balance on the scales of Libra.

DREAMBOY#3
Kansas plains would only stop this boy from running his
thoughts through her hair like a rear-view hijacker.

NORA
If 'yes' is a straight and narrow, the way Guinol means
'clown' but you thought it meant 'truth', then 'maybe' is the
dim filament of memory by which you piece together your
childhood like a ransom note and hold forth as sorcerer's
apprentice with nothing but confidence in your bag. You
called me Bel-Imperia. Belle de Jour. My love to you was a
utensil, an evil eye to keep yourself away.

OTHER MEN
When your Beast arrives
smelling like your father,
it will not knock politely
three times.

It scratches at the door until
a bloody posy rings around
the lead paint chips.
Don't invite it in from the rain,
wet, covered in mange from its
warthog laugh to its webbed toes.
You can't decide whether it's
more lion or fish.
Beneath its shaggy pelt
the bog peat smothered in
Tollund Men it comes
leaking the black marsh of
itself, festering bubbles
vent from iron-slit throat
the tarpit in its gizzard.
Between its twisted shanks, the
thistle of its undergrowth
prods a manly tuber, a
withered yam bald as the
thyrsus where a den of weasels
is conniving, sniffing and
crazy-wayed.
Don't seat it at the table.
Send your wife upstairs.
It picks a quail from its teeth, spits
out links of medieval chainmail.
Its trunk-like snout rummaging through
your pantry for termites.
Don't offer it milk or bread. It
wants ancient whiskey, steak
rare and red as young fear.

It demands a game, but you only have dominoes.
Smiling tarnished crockery, it curls up by the
hearth and leaves its coffee-dark stain under the
table by morning.

THE CRITIC
What will be the song that ended your career?

THE SALESMAN
When the harem-keepers finally call your tab?

THE MUSICIAN
When the next tantric child-bride in bathtub martinis
runs your red flag up the mast?

THE CRITIC
Did you swipe left on Potiphar's wife?

THE PHILOSOPHER
Can't decide whether you're Charlie Chaplin, James
Dean, or the prophet Jeremiah?

THE SALESMAN
Do you still pluck out your chest hairs and sell them
to fans?

THE MUSICIAN
Will you finally stop drinking when cracking open a
bottle feels like punching the clock?

THE CRITIC
Will your fame be protection when the beggars at the
gate all want to be you?

THE PHILOSOPHER
What would Darwin make of Hanuman? The divine
monkey who bit the sun like a casaba melon?

THE SALESMAN
Asbestos, Amway, breast implants a Coupe de Ville
red as too much lipstick

THE MUSICIAN
milking the sacred cow dry while telling her she is a lie.

*At the Monday night open mic Dreamboy#3 in a black
domino mask is reading poems about electroshock
therapy.*

THE CRITIC
Commedia dell'arte.

THE MUSICIAN
Lone Ranger.

THE PSYCHIATRIST
Is this funny?

THE CRITIC
How do you know enough to laugh?

THE MUSICIAN
Are you running from the law?

DREAMBOY#3
I am the law.

POLICEMAN
Am I you or me now?

OUTLAW
I don't know, did you get a check?

NORA
Apparently, I turn into a ghost and become translucent
whenever you're around. Either your vision is slowly
deteriorating or you're making a point not to cross paths with
me. Option A: If your vision is going you should see a doctor
immediately or get glasses, big goofy ones with huge lenses
and purple rims. Option B: If you are ignoring me, well…
don't.

DREAMBOY#3

Green ocean obsolete. No music as obscure as she.

NORA

Hey, thanks for the book and the conversation
and for guarding me from all those cars & geese…ish
and for spending the first night of
fall with me and for
being my friend
and for telling me it's okay to be in the
dark even though I was stubborn and for
revealing that you have vertigo
(or at least your leg does).
So, I guess what I'm saying is…
you're not half bad.
Just kidding.
G'night.

If you had a tea party, I would have come.
Or a chocolate party.
Or tapioca. But a lot of people don't like tapioca.
So would probably be just a me party. I'm excited.
We're having everything orange: cheese pizza (kind of
orange?), mangoes and Cheetos and carrots…I think
that's all we could come up with. Hmm.
How was your night?
P.S. Sorry I stole your sunglasses, I just think it's
amusing to watch you look around every time, like
you don't already know who took them. Yeesh.

I kind of want to be alone tonight. Today I found out. It reminded me when I first got my driver's license, just at the beginning of liberty, that first lick and tasting its terrifying glory. Driving into dark blue splattered with light, aimlessly, but even if I did, if I wanted to escape, I would still think about the same things, let them brew. Just let me know. Don't walk away from me just yet please. Realization, crying over the phone, so I ran back to Him and told him that I love him, and we got back together because that's what happens when two people belong together. Sometimes it takes a disaster to make a person realize what they really need in their life. If you feel robbed or hurt, I take all the blame and rightfully deserve it. I don't expect you to be happy for me. I'm sorry. I don't know what else to say.

DREAMBOY#3
I must spend time with you.
But can't.
I'm shy.
And you wouldn't be the person
that I'd planned for you to be.

Riddles Penultimate

A green tigress prowls, smokey-eyed, through the brass.
The Hammond organ hollers darkly from a nickel juke as
polyester divas clap over old beer and leather to hear the
muted trumpet. The chromium flume blows black and
blue, feelings scraped along gravel, aluminum cans, cigar
butts. The gold-tooth gambler said the word *jazz*
comes from *jasmine,* after the perfume worn by
prostitutes where Jelly Roll played piano. It moves him
to sport sharp threads, the pompadour, buoyant heeled,
rugs cut with fancy footwork, his luck greased down and
shining through two-tone spats, his bossanova alligators.

Yia-yia's Kashan rug from Smyrna, 1922.

Rubbing our noses in its field of saffron,
vineyards of illustration, we lay on our backs rolled in
opium dreamshapes inlaid as fine jewelry
from a Byzantine cathedral scattered on the floor.

A pomegranate ripens where the dried scab of the kermes
beetle bled her scarlet dye, her thorax trampled under six
hundred years of Greco-
Turkish feet.

Caressed by fingers of thread-cutters unspooling their fig-
bearing vines along the thorny rim of Anatolia stitched
together in dusky ages that
remember a flame the city wore as garlands of smoke.

Palmettes burn on the edge of our mothering blood woven
in lambswool.

Beneath me is the sycamore. I close my eyes to feed a
black ram breathing turmeric.

My cheek, borne aloft on a clutch of juniper stung by a
filigree prong, I slide along its woody tendril to a wasp's
nest of blackcurrants, mollusk shell splayed open, its airy
purse swollen with ovaries.

Side by side, our bodies fold into Persian
calligraphy.

She appears to me as a woman, but she may be a field
of saffron growing lush and rampant along the side of
embroidered mountains. Her hair, a tawny ruckus of
Indian henna emblazoned with gilded pinions dipped in
crocus petals that endow our spice-drenched carpet.

Or she may be the jazz of ambulance sirens.

Or some half-memorized passage from the Rubái-yát of
Omar Khayyám.

Or the taste of black licorice on her accent, a quart of rum
between us.

Now she tells me to undress. She'd discussed this with the
rum and it agreed. The rum was older and wiser than us
both.

It said,
"Beloved, taste of your own delightfulness!
Drink deeply!
Pray without ceasing!
Let blessing like sapphires drip
that you may you speak another tapestry!"

Unless a revolution comes…

…some Nazi Q-ball in the corner pocket
(basement-dwelling auteur with a wi-fi
connection) frat boy Heidegger baking the
universe from scratch gonna skim the Book of
Revelation every red pill YouTube video
accepted without question into his apocalyptic
gestalt scatting that Loompanics filibuster about
blood moons and Feast of Trumpets (Trumpets,
you see? This was all foretold!) counting down to
Judgment on the 23rd only to cower in his bunker by the 24th.

We Are Things in a Poet's House

The harmony of your pursed lips forms a tourniquet
between the weeks we are together
and the years we'll spend apart.

Friendship is a shard of glass that reflects everyone;
behaviors that rhyme with feeling.

They give me lemon egg drop soup and Debussy sheet music,
even though they know I can't play.
Objectification of sincerity.
They delight in creating me.

Running my thoughts through your hair like a comb,
teasing out braided moments, the spaces most dear to me
a little north of comprehension. Their mouths are full of light.

Depression is a blank. An addendum of bruises
underlined in the middle of the space you leave behind.
In the space that was once an object. This poem ends on
someone's anniversary, burrowed in your oriental rug,
the colors fall asleep.

The Bitching of Immaculate Jones

"Yessiree-bob, we had us a whale of a time! I think I
couldn't get enough of it down there. It's 'cuz I'm feeling
old. And every cat on the square's got some story to tell,
looking wet as a pup's nose. Still see the shine behind
those ears. 'Nuff said. Look, this ain't no thank you
card. Say, when's Ray getting laid? Last I heard, Mister
Man, he finally mustered enough brass to jump that new
bridge off Muskogee Lane. Hell, he'd sooner trap himself
in a broom cupboard than get with the likes of those
hometown sweethearts. Hardy har, ol' boy! If it was up to
me that knucklehead would've been up to his eyeballs in
Georgia Crockett's bosom long time ago. Come on
brother, be a good Samaritan and put your
quarters on the billiards. Help another weirdo
locate his mojo. Let it be known! He's got less than a
month's time, Mister Man, before that
saddle finds a new rider and picks up for that ol' sunset.
Rightly so. I feel a bit peaky these days. Feel like picking
a fight I know I'll lose. Mark my words, I am a sign of the
times, the one you've been waiting for. In fact I couldn't
tell you what we got up to that night. We met the whole
gang down there. There's Baby Ray, Jujube, Vida, Lit-tle
Dez, Fat Freddy, Rainbow Madge, Freewheel-in' Frank,
Mungo, Skitch, D-Trad, The Ginger. All flash and no cash
those kids. And Ray, he must've had with him thirteen
girls named 'Dul-cinea.' Bit o' luck on the geegees,
son. You ain't the first poet to been tied up by a woman.
Swin-burne, now he was a kinkster! 'Once
a philoso-pher, twice a pervert', as they say.

Even Rumi didn't like writ-ing but he'd cook some up when he had guests over. Ho, ho! You're in the groove now! Tickles me like a feather to my nethers! It's a vintage year for scoundrels, make no mistake! Margaret Fishback ain't got nothing on me, boy! Well, don't wanna keep you. Happy Crimbo! As I al-ways say, keep an eye on your shit, stay out of the restrooms and may your heart be as open as your wallet!"

Jessie Eikmann

Jessie Eikmann lives in south St. Louis, where she stocks shelves at a supermarket and occasionally screws around with writing. Though she mostly writes as a hobby these days, she spent six years obsessively devoted to poetry, culminating in her MFA from the University of Missouri-St. Louis in 2019. Her work has appeared in Sou'wester and Unbroken Magazine. Bad Jacket Press published a chapbook of her poems, The Kiss of Complicity, which she describes as "letters to all the people who disappointed me in my life." Jessie may or may not publish any more work soon, as she lacks professional ambition and does not care what content is "appropriate" for highbrow magazines. Post-MFA, she has spent most of her time cooking fancy vegetarian food, haunting her local gym, volunteering with her labor union and the Communist party, and seeking out various sexual dalliances on OKCupid.

Night Worker (Biopsy)

I keep warning white coats about the silence. There
are too few voices. A cough three aisles away is a
lightning bolt. A dropped box, the stunning thump
of ax to wood. Even the mice aren't talking. The
warehouse lights stagger on ahead of my steps, and
they run between pallets and under bunkers, no click,
no squeak, like plush toys dragged across the floor.
In the ragged afternoon, it was automatic to turn on
the monologue that twisted syntax and screwed pretty
little phrases into a board of belief. Now I dare not dent
the emptiness. The store's only voices are splintering
cardboard and shelves scraped by the lower lips of cans.

My doctors are not amused. They brush off my
pleading, say how peaceful or how liberating. As if they
prescribed the silence. As if they packaged it in a pill
and paired it with my uppers (espresso, ten p.m.) or my
downers (sedatives, eleven a.m.) And on a separate pad:
new companions. Wonder Woman leans seductively
in front of Coke cubes. A fake doo-wop group cuts
into the loudspeaker music every two hours, singing
swe-e-e-EET Northwest Che-er-ries so happily you can
hear the jazz hands they don't have. Ten tumescent
Katy Perrys in salmon jumpsuits follow me along the
wall. *The Globe* mourns "faces we lost in 2020." They
claimed to lose Kenny Rogers. I lost everyone I knew
in daylight.

Off nights, I wander the street and the light is all
wrong. Harsh, glossy, like a magazine page. Through
heavy blinking I watch the sun trip over the tool shed
and conjure up my backyard. I am surprised to see
it—white wicker patio chairs, wooded back edge and
its low-hanging phone wires, tree that died five years

ago yet persists like a split, wrinkled maypole—perfectly replicated every day. The day will come, I'm certain, when the magic trick goes awry and a moss-matted castle or merry-go-round will await me instead.

I dare my doctors to write that on their pads. I dare them to stop handing me forms and go straight to pricking. They'll wait for blood and get nothing. They'll stare at the air stoppered in the syringe and shrug. Their heart monitor will stop searching me and play back proof of their own vitality instead. I dare them to lean in my empty eyes, tell me I'm healthy. I dare myself to believe it.

The hospital's note
brought to my bed: *you're not sick*
enough to stay here.

"Rodeo Style Bedroom Antics"

What are those, exactly?
What are you picturing?
Do you think I'm rubbing
a gun muzzle
against my boyfriend's beard,
or ending every sexual exclamation
with *howdy, pardner,*
or slapping a saddle on him &
making him buck under me
on his carpet?
There are no holsters,
no horseshoes,
no straw strung between teeth,
no cigarettes, even.

Tonight I stand before a glass door,
strutting in my Jockeys
& imagining myself
kicking in those swinging saloon
double doors, blowing
into the piano player's lap
while he tickles both the ivories
& my chin--& if any hombre
complains about his entertainment
being interrupted,
or tries to snarl *hey dollface,*
I got something to fill

that hat of yours,
I'll chomp the tops off
bottles & spit ground glass
in his eyes saying
call me sir.

But this is all a charade,
a pageant masking
the only math problem that matters:
how many goddamn birthdays
do I have to add to twenty-five
before a sixty-something man
with a Ph.D. stops seeing me
as a wayward little girl?

I Wish I'd Failed at Glassblowing

You write that at least I'm not a glassblower.
Our trade can wait forever.   It requires no rentals
and its equipment is so easily slipped
in a purse. *There's nothing*
you will need to sell, cancel,   or shut down.
I make that sentiment
brittle with rebuttals.   I sell my body,
                    but not that way,
transactions with boxes   and plastic   and blunted blades
that score my forearms,   re-split
the same knuckle, make me think someone   unearthed
my vertebrae   and sanded pieces   off them.
    22,000 steps
    a night, half on a heel   that screams   if I linger
          on that leg.   I shut down,
                    but not that way,
intransitive.   Mostly my nights are
that person reminds me of   [STOP]
that debris on the street looks like   [YOU'RE
that phrase could title a   FINISHED WITH
                              THIS] [THE BALER
                              HAS NO EARS, BUT
                              THE COWORKER
                              THAT JUST CAUGHT
                              YOU TALKING TO
                              YOURSELF SURE
                              DOES]

And the glassblower?
Think of all that she can blame for her failure.
       The workshop maintenance, the customers
       fussing over a vase that they want,
           but not that much,
       unanswered prayers from the almighty
       dollar.   I have no scapegoat,
           just the sad sack that scours her teeth
               in concert with me every morning
               and says she is "semi-retired"
           from art
           at 27.
I wish I'd failed at
           art that was real,
           art that matters
to people without Ph.D.s because it's
           something you could feel.
The ridges,   the hollows,   the little bits of grit
that sometimes survive the fire and the scrutiny after.
So unlike our lines, it's
           something we could shatter,
and even with harsh light   and harsher eyes,
             the fragments on the floor
               might still sparkle.

Brian, the Bread Guy: A Letter

I am introduced to my friend's bread guy
as he sets up his selections at the farmer's market.
I am free to discuss any of them: his biscotti, his scones,
his breakfast burritos so perfectly insulated in foil.
But I'm not allowed to talk about the woman lurking
above his stand. Miss Shure,
his soon-to-be ex-wife, printed in dollar-bill green
and lording it over the loaves like the goddamn Mona Lisa.
And if anything, she seems a bored or downright disgusted
spokeswoman, because she won't look
at the buyer or the wares. Something more interesting
must be in the banner's top left corner.
My friend won't let me express condolences,
so I keep my lips and eyes from saying, *I'm sorry
you got duped too* or *it will get better after.* But really,
what the hell do I know? Not enough. That this Shure
tries to stand in front of his own ovens at night.
That he'll have to excise her from everything:
the market stall signs, business cards, menus—
even the business name is branded with his betrayer.

I won't say you were a peach about our parting.
You dumped me like used charcoal in my dad's driveway,
waved your white-collar money in my face. I'm still paying
for the brand you left, in money and in perennial sheets of
scabs on my shoulder. I'll say instead
that I was fortunate. What a gift it is to be

a non-entrepreneur, a no-name composer, insulated
by a big city. I thought myself so wretched then.
I did the pitiful victim's song and dance, but the worst it got
was clutching the lid of a spaghetti sauce jar in shock
when I turned and found you right behind me.
Can you imagine if every poem I printed
was on stationery headed with that picture
of you in your silky white dress
inspecting your lipstick on our wedding day?
Or if, every time my fingers clicked out a word,
you picked up my wrist and slapped it back on my lap?
I thank you for your non-presence, for fleeing and leaving me
in a place where the dirt someone flung on your face
isn't even remarkable. In a town like yours, or Brian's,
people remember who isn't next to you in bed
or at the market. No, you let me off easy.
I only hope that you don't have new reasons to hide
in small town Wisconsin, and that someday when Brian
hands off his pastries, he won't feel he's selling
the idea of his ex.

How We Play House

My wife is making her favorite fruitcake.
She lines up our metal mixing bowls, pudding cloth,
    foil, our soup pot.
She goes to the pantry for the brown sugar, opens the
    container,
and frowns.

> *I'm not sure I can use this.*
> *Yeah,* I say, *it's a brick isn't it?*
> *I found that out when I made oatmeal this*
> *morning. Probably should have told you*
> *earlier. Damn,* she says, *I guess I'll have to get*
> *more. But first, I need to wash those dishes.*

She can't resist looking back
as she sings over the faucet,
> *Having fun?*
My only answer is a hum. I am falling in love with
my boyfriend's ear, my nose following
every little ridge and lingering over the lobe,
wanting to whisper something,
but this newness defies eloquence. I sit
on his lap as far as the armchair
will allow, back against the armrest and skirt
bunched aside but not discarded.

His hands swipe my thigh,
but he won't take off anything of mine, only
pulls his sweatshirt halfway off.

He hesitates and the shirt
tumbles over his head
once my wife turns from
tracing a plate with a sponge
and nods. Our lips touch and we decide
this is urgent,
we need more room to close
what small space is left between us.
I don't even wait to strip naked
until I get to the bedroom. My clothes
are thrown at random
on the living room floor.

Before the bedroom door closes,
mock astonishment called down the hallway,
> *Hon, did you really throw your bra in the pantry?*
As she hands it through the door
I analyze her face, her voice, looking for
sharpness, bitterness, irony.
I find none, and my boyfriend laughs
from the bed. This doesn't even feel
real to *me,* and I arranged all this.
How is it possible
that more than one person
can love you like that?

The Happy Genius in the Kitchen

after Danse Russe

Every day I laugh
at my hopelessly unraveled,
useless apron, unravel myself
(khakis, shirt, bra, socks, underwear
if I'm feeling ambitious),
and cook dinner.
It's just as icky
as you'd expect:

vegetable pieces
jumping down and slapping
my bare thighs and invading
anywhere I sit and
anywhere I step
with carrot ends;
curls of celery,
or the slimy scabs
of potato skin;

my hand slipping
and vegetable stock
or soy sauce
or half-and-half
getting splashed
on the tapestry
of my breast;

garlic's scent sneaking
into every unexpected
fold of my body
that clothes would cover;

oil sparks
kissing my groin
before I can duck away.

But even though
I push a slotted spoon
through that oil
thinking *someday*
I will shrink myself
to fit through holes,
someday I will be weightless,

and even though I always
sit contemplating
what I've made,
fiddle with the rim
of the plate, and realize
the sad absurdity
of that wish—

I dare you to tell me
that this sensory assault
is incongruous with joy,
or I don't love food,
or food doesn't love me.

With the first fairy flick
of salt in water
I conjure up
perfect, shining
shards of color,
a canopy of heat,
a soundscape rich with
rasp and sibilance,
and in that world
I am, in fact, weightless.

Escorting at Planned Parenthood

I've been donning my Velcro vest & plastic whistle
for a few weeks now, & I must confess
I was about ready
to blow this pop stand.
So when your friend with the ferret face
showed up today to film the escorts,
I just thought: Why?
There's nothing happening here.
It's a few seconds of wild gesticulation
at a closed SUV window—you waving
a pamphlet & me flailing
my arms inward
like those dudes on airplane runways—
& then dead air. A staring
contest between gate bars.
What Ferret Face really captures here
is our struggle as the triangle players
in our orchestras.
& as he puts down the iPad
& flops back in his lawn chair waiting
for the next car, I marvel that
we obsess over the same glob
of cells while it sits
oblivious in a dark pink castle.
Every week my whistle gets less breath.
Are you also bored
with our jingling? Do you ever just wish

somebody would win
so you could pack your sandwich board
back into your bus across the street
& we can get our medals or whatever &
go home?

Self Portrait: Old Woman on a Cruise Ship

The second your toe touches the boards
on the deck, you are assaulted by a line
of youngsters in white suits, cherubs shouting over the swell
of staged laughter from passengers. They wave
you down and you're desperate to bolt.
You see yourself reflected in their pristine teeth,

your horrified eyes and bared teeth
desperate to find a diving board
off this thing before your cabin's deadbolt
clicks and you're expected to fall in line
and participate in "activities," smile and wave
for brochure pictures, lie that *everything's swell*

on postcards you send friends. You'd rather swell
against someone's body, collect their scratches and teeth
marks, make them dig until they hit water, waves
way better than the dinky things sloshing against the boards.
They told you you're too old for this life of pickup lines
and sideways eyes. Now that your hips have bolts,

they suggest "hobbies" and send you here so you can bolt
down a Cornish hen dinner and quell your swelling
dread with wine tastings and lounge singers, line
dancing, bridge, the counterposed teeth
and rigid boxes of the shuffleboard
court, looking down when your "friends" wave

and beckon. Might as well try the waves,
disrupt the paddleboard lesson and stand bolt
upright, plunge off your board,
and drown. You'll finally get to swell,
though with sea water. The salt will lodge in your teeth
like the *it's not your fault* line

he fed you when he abstained. No lifeline
in the world could pull you from those waves
of betrayal, disgust, your teeth
pressed together when you think of his legs bolted
shut and your stagnant blood that will never swell
again. You'll hop on the "hobby" horse, board

your body up, let it shrivel into lines of skin, bolts
of bones. Once you waive your urges, organs swell,
spine shrinks, teeth rot. The body's response to being bored.

Non-Aubade, Post Separation

                        the guard is practicing boxing
                        on a utility pole
he bounces to the left
                and sneaks behind it
                        with a right fist,
then switches hands   every minute
                        the pole persists
                        he rages and
                                pumps his fist
                                        one more time before
                        releasing

                the hag wrapped
                        in greasy glass lets her
                        cigarette shrink
                                in her fingers
                while she laughs
                        or fails to breathe

                I'm tired of waiting for buses
                        for the hearing
                                for a disaster
                                for the lumped lazy sky
                                        to want to do anything
                                        I need it
                        to rattle the windows
                                unscrew the wavering

streetlight so it strikes
        my skull

    how long
    before the guard's knuckles connect
    and bleed   or the woman's lungs
             somersault from her throat

how long before these bruises are visible?

Aubade, Post-Divorce

I see dendrites splitting their backs. Leaves, only red
leaves. But the wide-eyed woman stepping on the metro
points at the piles on the floor. "Roses!" she laughs. "How
magical!" I want to slap her. The trees dumped these
here to remind me love is everywhere, abundant and
indiscriminate and sickening. I refuse to watch them and
instead watch a line of streetlights abandon my eyes.

Nature doesn't give gifts. Animals can't stand to look at
you. Weeds punch their heads furiously through dirt
regardless. Sun leaves your skin whipping-red. Even the
stars' *look at me, look at me* flamboyance is a construct,
since they're all dead. These things don't care that you
exist. They don't hand you thimbles of river water and
invite you to swallow. They don't whisper to you that
all petals lavished at a lover's feet are destined to be
stepped on. But I want to be with them, roll over floor
grit, let them leave pink prints on my body, point at the
stains as proof of pain. This train needs to slow down,
go backwards even. Just a few more seconds to choke on
bitter liquid. A few more seconds to feel something.

S. Elizabeth Cook

S. Elizabeth Cook is an award-winning author and poet of four published poetry collections, the most recent being Yellow Light. A true romantic, S. Elizabeth has spent nearly a decade writing about and capturing the raw existence of humans, nature and love. She believes there is beauty in heartache and a deflating pain in love, and that one must fall to let it hurt.

Vagabonds, Truckers and Romantics

Storms that claim limestone off the ports of Maine,
dragging stone chip by chip and pebble by pebble
back to the sea.

Interstates and highways - home to vagabonds,
    truckers and romantics -
giving mile after mile and turn after curve of
    themselves until
blood and sand is all that remains.

And I, all that is me, pick and pick
piece by piece and then heaps and heaps
until the skin is torn and raw.
And all that is left is none that makes me.

What more, and more
and more
do you need?
What could we give
and give
and give that you would take
and keep?

After rain

After rain,
street lights shine like diamonds on the road.
Where demons disperse, crawl back home
to Lucifer - laughing and singing
stories of slaughter and lust
we kept hidden.

Forgive me, lover, for I have sinned.

After rain,
I am a ghost to her and she is a ghost to me.
Crows circle around after the storm -
ready to pick bones and tongues long with lies
from the ground.

After rain,
once the Earth is rid of war and us,
demons lie in wait -
ready to return again.

Arrest or Unrest

A swollen Kentucky sky
wakes slow and sure over
rain stained red brick and still
puddles on pavement.

Like glitter in the light,
a faint morning dew
creeps through the city.

But, not a rain or thunder exists
that could wash these
streets clean—
could wash them of us.
We will stick longer than
warm, stolen blood.

You can still hear the rhapsody
of our heels pressed firm
in the ground. A pulse of
community louder than
gospels in empty cathedrals.
We are the sound of a distant drum,
beating in our chest.
Feeding our lungs with promises
of a breath at rest.

Somewhere in California

The blood boiled in a still sea.
As far as one could see,
curtains of crimson steam
covered the night.

Sharks, like knights jeweled for war,
came out to feed.

Clouds seemed like misty eyes,
waiting in the sky, watching over us.
Wavering before they pour.

If this is to end in fire and smoke,
as the ash weighs our lungs,
pick our bones from their teeth.

Hold Me Tight

Here it comes again.
A Sunday sun, another morning
pulling me from sleep
just in time to see it dusted across your cheeks.
Painting your skin
with blurred colors of picked wild flowers
wet with dew.
I am jealous of the light
how close it gets to you,
the way it dances through your freckles
as if clumsy fingers comb through stars
on an autumn night.

Here it comes again.
Waiting to wake, careful with my breath.
Waiting for your eyes to peek through
the breaks of the sun.
Waiting for them to find me in the shadows of
our sheets,
to touch me, and still my envy.

Here it comes again.
The sigh of relief jumping from my chest
as you close the space between our skin,
when our limbs and lips are tangled tight.

French Quarter

I.
The week held tight to Tuesday afternoon,
spreading butter on the clock while
trumpets sang in the streets of the Quarter.

II.
A promise of rain and rolling purple skies above us as
we danced off beat and beads of sweat and
colored jewels adorn her.

III.
After time has melted and boiled down, when
dusk greets dawn and it all wakes with vigor and might
    once more...

IV.
...we will return late.
For the sheets held tight to her body—wearing only my hands
and the grey light of morn.

A Whiskey, Fever Dream

Eyes and tongue so wild
with the light of the morning sun, but
she burns like ice in the rain when they fall on me.
I threw myself in the fire to feel her breathing.

I found her lungs sleeping peacefully in the cold,
biting my hands for reaching in the frost.

Darling, she moves beneath you
like sheets thawing after Winter takes a final bow.

Are you watching?
Her bones break over you like twigs of dying trees,
    covering the bed
with leaves left to freeze on the ground.

Soft as Prayers

Her skin, like marble,
is etched with Testaments
I will weave between
my fingers.
I will call her name
out like gospel.

Drips of promises,
soft as prayers,
will fall from my tongue
on to hers.

Sura

She was the sun never to rise again.
A heavy thing mere lands could not dare hold still.
The grounds now weep, cloaked with damp leaves.
The smell of decay fills and swells the breath of air.
Skies, black and weary, tremble with ache;
when puddles, like shattered glass, catch in the starlight
you can almost see the ghost of her warmth.
We were the night never to wake again.
A sour sleep leaving us restless still.

Spartacus, Bringer of Rain

Heavens split to bring a rain with
dreams to grant fertile soil.
In hopes grounds will break open
and forge a new body after legions in her hands
ripped it from this Earth.

See the way clouds cry, imploring return
of intended path carved from my heels.
It will greet but a pale shadow
of a life once drawing breath
that hailed gusts and tides to rival Poseidon himself.

She placed lungs and spirit upon a pyre
and watched ash find itself
lost among errant winds.

Mira

Hands tried to bend sheets around a stranger's skin,
legs fared frozen when tangled in foreign limbs.
What is of use this body,
where is it meant to roam, to land, to settle
now that yours has crumbled to blood and sand beneath
    my feet?

Does my tongue bare meaning when names absent yours
    spill from parted lips?
No, it becomes filled with empty desires and faith.

Break open my head and see thoughts
lost, scurrying to find an inch where you still remain.

Once, these eyes were sweetened with sights of you to chart
    through.
See them now eclipsed with the retreat of
color in the sun, and
you far from reach.

Little House

Like little sirens I never heard,
the breaks in your breath now fill my
head with white noise on the road back
to this little house.

Collected dust settles on empty chairs
at empty tables.

Walls with paint chipping from your skeletons poking out.
Humidity after the storm coats my mouth,
but my voice never held any weight on your ears,
did they?

I watched this little house crumble to sand,
as all fortresses before it.
As my knees fell to prayer, shattering my bones,
trying to land on steadier ground before you.

Miles, and my bones, stretch across damp skies. Skin tight
    under tired eyes.
Heavy with the frayed promises on your tongue.
The clouds split for the rainfall as your
promises fell like hope in empty cathedrals.

A Canvas of Delicately Stitched Freckles
and Muscles

That back.
A canvas of delicately stitched freckles and muscles.
Tied to her spine, keeping her in place. Keeping her close.
    I loved to explore her back.
Trailing tips of my fingers along
mountains that held minutes and mornings she spent
    gliding through this air.
I watched her leave on the first night
the moon hovered above the both of us. Through a fog of
    curiosity, hesitancy and tequila, her back pulled my
    eyes home with her.

My lips found a groove when they pressed
against the skin of her back that peeked from the sheets.
    Covered in sweat, Sunday laze and me,
her back rolled to greet me, pull me from sleep. I felt her
    stir on top of me,
her back moving beneath my palms, my body moving
    beneath her.
I walked out through her door before dusk,
waiting for another dawn where her back tucked, and
    nestled into my chest.

That back.
It carried the weight of our shoulders, and the weight of
    her secrets.

I watched them spill out.

Leaving puddles on my door step, soaking my feet.

I looked down to catch the reflection of her back
    leaving in the night. Leaving, this time, for good.
    The water dried, taking her reflection with it.

The image lingered; the image lingers.

I see her back whenever my eyes catch the sun;
    whenever my eyes catch a light,

I see her walking from me once more.

That back.

A canvas of delicately stitched freckles and muscles.
    With dried brushstrokes of my touch,

peeling away morning after morning.

Debris

Steadily tucked away,
sat a loaded gun;
quietly and readily
behind your tongue
aimed for me.

A ringing in my ears
rattled my skin,
crushed my bones.
I floated in the smoke
crawling from your mouth; ashes to fill your lungs.

What did you sift
through your teeth?
What was left whole of me
to swallow?

Miles and Miles

The Heavens spoke to Gabriel
with words that floated through dawn.
Coursing through winds, dripping hymnals in the rain.

Paving the interstates between us,
stripping away the dry roads
that dehydrate my breath.
Bring me miles and miles
of you, let me pile my hands
and my lips atop your skin.

Baptize my throat, make space to
swallow, "I miss you," and shout,
"I see you."

Bring me mornings
with wrapped sheets and legs,
and I will fall to my knees
to sing to the Heavens again.

So loud the gates will break open — never to close
    behind me with
you on the other side.

Definition of Morning

What is morning if not her
fingers clumsily decorating my skin?
If not my lips, wild and full of whispers, shoveling
    through the sheets
to pull her from sleep?
If this air is not swollen with sweat, not drenched
    with her breath,
do not wake me. Leave me to my dreams.
They are woven with blonde strands of
her hair lost on my pillow.
Left behind to remind me of the artful mess of her
    body spread alongside mine.
If I am tangled in this, I am both held
together and torn apart.
I will empty my beaten chest to fill her hands.

Never will I crawl from bed.
Never could time peel my mouth from hers.

Wayfaring Drunk

Kaleidoscopes at the bottom of bottles,
turning glazed eyes to stars, shaping the sky to bend
    around my skin.

The quiet, bouncing off desolate streets,
sing a lullaby that teases my sleep.
The fog— it notices the absence of her breath that
    once leaned against my neck— it tries to
fill my chest.

But the smoke will clear, the bottles will run
dry, and I will still hear
a screaming halt; I will still see
empty sheets too loud for me to rest.

Hands

She was the type of love poets spent
rum soaked nights wrapping her in pages.
Dipping her in half used ink to fill her with words
of how she filled their sheets.
But, here I am, stumbling
over my own fingers, forgetting
I had hands that never held hers.

Birds of Indianapolis

The birds chirped,
lifted their wings in awe,
to wake the sleeping city.
In applause
for her fingers taking
flight across my morning skin.
Those lips calling me from rest,
gripped my neck. I filled
her hands — she filled my breath.
We descended into disheveled sheets,
 found home in a broken bed.
I gathered my bones, and her lost curls, to
build a nest on top of her chest.
My shaking voice and
fleeting eyes learned to land on her.

Mack Thorn

Mack Thorn is poet from St. Louis, Missouri. Growing up he has lived in almost every corner, nook, and cranny of his home town. Worked a broad array of conventional and unconventional jobs like drug rehabilitation and dry wall hanging. He also spent 6 years in the navy reserve. Published works in *Badjacket* zine and the *Whiskey Rye Review.*

Deliverance

To some,
deliverance wasn't just a movie
but a manifesto.
The way nature seeks repentance
from man and the unjust contract.

The sacrifice was made
and some mistakes too.
Offer my life as tribute
to the mother river.
This natural menace
this orgy of death
plots against us.

The bugs and trees ferment plans of reprisal
through trickles and tiny beating wings
that hum against the smooth rocks.
These toads seem to be in on it too
jumping from their spider holes
like slimy freedom fighters
in an anticipation of what's to come.

This rusted old fence
is the closest thing to an ally I have out here.
All besides that guy on a ski doo
skipping down the river
he seems pretty alright.

Cowboy Poetry

Cowboys on horseback
glide and thunder across the terrain.
Noble like forefathers
rugged and cold
manifestations of divine will.

They crossed the ridgeline
and over the horizon
to greet the refugees
with whips and the word of God.

Corral and rustle poor souls
from the shifting sand.
Nets thrown like fishers of men and Jesus in tow.
Their tears were the first drops of rain seen in months.

There is no room at the inn
my dear Mary.
The savior of man
will not be born today
nor anytime soon.

Wild Dogs

Eyes swell in passenger seats,
and husking breath shackles the ribcage.
Some indie pop song,
bursting through one speaker
because the rest have been broken by abuse.

The air in conversation,
awaits in stillness
Interrupted by passing car.

Then,

out from one side of the field,
wild dogs emerge from the darkness.
A pack of many
ranging in all sizes
roll in hunger across the wild grass.

Their calloused paws drum the rotten earth.
Marching towards the battle against the hoof and lone
    sorry souls.
Untrimmed nails clicking against the concrete,
with glinting eyeballs that lick against the white lights
    of mankind.

Let them pass,
this horde of fur doesn't quarrel with metal frame beasts.

Put it in drive
and render this asphalt pasture to its rightful owners.

let's talk about this tomorrow,
I say with foggy breath.
Spared from a thunderstorm of fangs
and conversations that can't be finished in parked cars.

3 AM

At 3 AM
when typing away
or swinging madly at guitar strings
and drumming piano keys.

One must have red wine
and red meat.
Be it pork,
or beef,
dried,
cured,
or cooked.

Wipe not the grease from fingers
but apply to brow
and keyboard.

As evidence
for the morning doubt
that will surely come.

But if I'm being frank
don't call me surely
call me drunk.

Maybe This Just Ain't for Me

Smiles eclipsed by runaway mascara.
Freshwater springs born from the divine iris
swell
and
grow.
The pillars of Greece bow at your spiked heels.

Maybe this just ain't for me,
alleyway rivers
dispose of stand by saints.
Limbs made from cut steel
demand life from flesh.

Your promises left out overnight
forgotten until the flies make claim.
Come on cowboy take the poison,
If it's the divine you seek
take the drink
but I never said
I wanted to die in southeast Kansas.

Midnight Special

Play Otis Redding
and set my coffin adrift along the river Styx.
I can't see nothing beneath this crescent moon.
April breeze lets me know I'm not alone
as it swims between reflections of familiar strangers.

I cry,
why
was I
the one.

Five-dollar red wine
and candles glowing soulful harmonies.
Sweat-stained pillowcase dresses
clenched until knuckles turn white.
Cigarettes set adrift at red lights after midnight.
Green onions growl black coal exhaust.
Red meat juice cools warm red lips.
Manic pirouettes blossom orgasm tantrums.

Rejoice,
the son has returned.

Camelot

Bruschetta
shared upon the table,
draped in olive oil
and adorned in salt and pepper.

Smoke lingers and ribbons
between smiles fractured from corner pockets.
Commercial interruptions for disgruntled flaccid
    boomers
intrigue and dismay.
Laughter like slashing sword,
brought down on the necks of boredom.

Calls for gas station pilgrimages
amass sugar crusades.
The march towards the holy land comes with icy
    gasping breath.
Infidels to us and
infidels to them.
The pillage brought great bounty
and the journey home begins.

Fortunes told of this great conquest
upon sticky palms and
stories of old will quiver at our name.
King Arthur and his round table can go fuck himself.
These slackers and their coffee table
shall be the halls to be remembered.

Dusk in a Sundown Town

It gets dark so fast now,
the bats don't feel the need
to flicker against the dusk.

There is more night to go around
enough sunken moon to chew
and stars consumed through straws.

Like a milkshake
we all sit here and enjoy it.
Taking turns dipping fries into the sauce
lamenting in the moments we have before
 the coming frost
or floods to come.

High Hill Missouri

The small 10 by 15 box truck drove down the gravel road at
    high speed.
Hugging the turns so much you could feel the g force pulling
    at the top end of the truck
Like a bear, prying open the cab
to pull us down into the jaws of the green abyss below.
There were three of us in the cab.
Tim the foreman was driving, myself in the middle, and
    Topher to my right.
After driving up and down the perilous back roads of the
    Missouri highlands
for what seemed like gasping moments of forever.
The truck was spat in a level clearing
and just as we broke the tree line
3 am by Matchbox Twenty began to play on the radio.
Tim went cold
then drew in a sharp breath
like a tornado about to touch down on the plains.
Possessed by the music
that mad bloodhound began to bellow each word of the song.
Every line leaped from his toothless mouth and then past
    his bushy red mustache
In a lonely howl
calling out to his former soul.

He said once before that, he had lost his teeth in a prison
    fight over drug debt
and nowadays they can give you a pretty good new set
    of ivories on the inside.

More likely,
they rotted from years of neglect and mountain dew
but the first is a better story.
Both of his hands were gripping the wheel with such
 intensity
that he might just rip it off the dashboard.
Only letting go
to occasionally take a drag from his maverick full
 blend cigarette.

THREE AM I MUST BE LONELY
The chorus cried into the Midwestern wilderness.

His voice sounded like a newspaper being stuffed
 down a garbage disposal
from decades of chain smoking at 3 A.M.
But
at that moment,
nothing else mattered to him but that song and the
 memories with it.
At that moment
he wasn't in the truck or in high hill Missouri
heading towards a job site
for a company that doesn't pay enough.
He was in a better place
as a better version of himself.

Beer Kegs and Foxholes

We were talking to spirits amongst the gopher holes.
Tripping over rocks and gaining strength from leaning on
    headstones.
Diving headfirst into the red brick jungle with pale
    florescent faces.
The road we roam leads to nowhere and this alleyway is
    just another dead end.

When you're all alone you take any kind of friend you can get.
That's how we got here,
It's better to be close to death with a friend than drunk and
    alone.
Begging for grace in the face of God by shooting pistols
    straight at the sky.

I remember that backyard kingdom of roses.
Bullet holes and creek frog songs,
dagger style smiles drawn with speed like switchblades.
Gather the troops for the fire pit release.
Cases, kegs, and dancing flames fondle membranes of
    spreading legs

We didn't have much promise for a future
nor did we try and dream for one.
Hope is a waste of time when you could just be getting
    wasted instead.
But here we are ten years later,
blocks away from the fox holes we dug in a hurry.

Vortex

I sat down at the dimly lit daytime barroom.
Greeted kindly by barstool neighbor and bartender
worked for too hard and long.
I watched the old flat tops at the bar play five finger dice
because the gaming machine wasn't giving up the juice
like it usually does.
The barflies hover in Marlboro light smoke and
reminisce over Andy Griffith days.

I figure things here haven't changed much over the years.
A time vortex hiding out along the interstate.
If they leave, they might turn to dust.
Basking in the television for news from the mainland.
As far as I have gathered,
the only thing different to the old days is when they
changed the draft from stag to miller lite.

I could see myself running away to a place like this.
A place where you can't feel the world spin.
just the wagon wheel turning from day to night
hungry or full,
drunk or dry.
Inside a cabin filled with dust and empty wine bottles,
rummaging through a box of nick knacks looking for
something I could have sworn was in there.
Can't help but wonder where the time went
But if the world outside doesn't exist
I won't pay it no mind

Country Roads is About the Western Part of Virginia

Roaming the countryside
upon my noble metal steed.
Its belly grumbles and rolls
churning gears and bolts.

The radio doesn't work
and neither does the ac,
but as long as the windows roll down
in this fall air, I don't mind.

John Prine tells me about small towns,
clocks and scales,
plaster hiding holes with rye whiskey,
and women that only last the night
from a cellphone speaker sitting bitch.

Cascades of brown, yellow, and green
infect my behind the wheel daydreams.
Surrounded by rolling hills and slow rivers
like Napoleon at Borodino
I take on all invaders.

Take my hand off the reign only to wave three fingers
at oncoming locals.
Floral canopy tunnels serve as bridges between hollers.

No trespassing signs
and curious bovines
all gander at my noble commute.

An alien stranded upon an alien world
making the best
of what the best has to offer

Maggie's Peanut Gallery

You give life
Iike the Ganges River
poisoned by own hand
and rotting flesh.

Here at Maggie's peanut gallery,
entrance is free but release comes with a price tag.
These gold teeth ain't cheep
but neither is being this cool.

This white light is so hot
It's melting my sunglasses.
Good thing I'm friends with the Texas sun
and she owes me a favor or two

When I was a boy
all I knew were wide wheel cyclones
driving slow around potholes
shiny like silver capped teeth.

Box chevy chariots
hovering around parking lots and one way stops
the schoolgirl buzzards
wait…

The first time I saw a Lamborghini
it was bright green and clean

no cavities or decay
as I wiped bagel bite grease from my face
and clutched my rat tail
the man opened his window and said,

you go to school, and you'll have one of these someday

that'll be the day
replied my fiscal fate.

Just Another Scene

Just a bunch of crusty skid marks
getting old in a basement together.
Giving out GHB in stag stockings
to unaware
manic pixie teenage girls.
Nobody cares
about your crescent moon face tattoo
and nobody wants your stepped on coke.
Go take another tab
and carry these shingles up that roof
you bum.

Port by the Gallon

Drinking port by the gallon under crumbling barn skylight.
The sugar blisters our gums and dulls our senses.
It tastes like a smooth talker that shaves his face
and walks away arm in hand with the girl of your dreams.

This is the first day of fall of that which we both agree.
Our iris graced by the orange splendor
It's not the end of melatonin season just yet
but I can hear winter beating its wings in the distance

I speak in fermented grape
and you're beginning to learn by ear and liver.
English starts to turn into layered code
by which we understand in dermis brail.

If my heart could fly like a store-bought kite
drawn by thin string and tangled by its own design.
The wind picking up my cross-stick frame
towards the Simpson's style blue sky and clouds.

The hawks, buzzards, and crows pay little attention.
A stupid bald eagle might take it on
dive bomb from the middle of a cloud
mistaking my heart for a meal.

Your last check was blown on gimps and leather masks.
They huddle under your porch light scratching at the back door.

Praying for a chance to be graced by your heel and spit.
Leashed by the collar of your halo and grateful for the abuse.

Your dominion over man is only at its genesis
and this world is your drooling Eden.
Take one last sip of scenery
before we get back to the gravel.
Before the sun runs from the moon.

It seems that these are the last of the sunny days
before the winter air makes some legroom.
The last of
the best days ahead of us.

This project was made possible, in part, by generous support from the Osage Arts Community.

Osage Arts Community provides temporary time, space and support for the creation of new artistic works in a retreat format, serving creative people of all kinds — visual artists, composers, poets, fiction and nonfiction writers. Located on a 152-acre farm in an isolated rural mountainside setting in Central Missouri and bordered by ¾ of a mile of the Gasconade River, OAC provides residencies to those working alone, as well as welcoming collaborative teams, offering living space and workspace in a country environment to emerging and mid-career artists. For more information, visit us at www.osageac.org

Osage Arts Community